Steph Chaplen lives in Hampshire with her two cats, Pickles and Asher. She has recently taken up voluntary work for a local organisation. Steph enjoys writing and painting in water colours, doing mostly flowers and landscapes during her travels. She has raised money for various charities including RNLI, Cat Protection League and Samaritans.

To Jen
from
Steph x

This book is dedicated to the memory of my dear friend, Kay.

Steph Chaplen

A BATTLE OF WITS!

AUSTIN MACAULEY PUBLISHERS™

LONDON · CAMBRIDGE · NEW YORK · SHARJAH

A CIP catalogue record for this title is available from the British Library.

ISBN 9781035830572 (Paperback)
ISBN 9781035863198 (ePub e-book)

www.austinmacauley.com

First Published 2024
Austin Macauley Publishers Ltd®
1 Canada Square
Canary Wharf
London
E14 5AA

My mum in loving memory.

My cousin Ginny and Aunty Marilyn for support.

My consultant for listening to me.

Parkway Centre, Crisis Team, Safe Haven for support when I needed it.

My cats for just being there.

Music that has inspired me.

Carpenters, Mylie Cyrus, Shirley Bassey, Cilla Black, Elton John, Abba.

Prologue

This book is about the changes that came about going from one depot to another and the progresses that I made.

Suddenly, my life was opening up to new possibilities and a new start.

Almost a moment-to-moment account of life as it is now.

I have included the titles of songs that have inspired me.

IF AT FIRST YOU DON'T SUCCEED, TRY, TRY, TRY AGAIN!

Chapter One
The Beginning

If you've never had a Schizoaffective Disorder, then you won't understand what I go through day after day. One day feeling absolutely fine, going along nicely, then WHAM, everything goes hay wire again. It's a battle of wits to keep going. I struggle at first, then the depression takes a hold. It's like it goes from the top of my head down to my feet!

'At the moment it's resting on my shoulders but I know
It's just a matter of time before it reaches my feet –
Then I'm in trouble. No eye contact, no make-up, no
Drive, no ambitions, no way forward.'

Firstly, it was put on a depot (injection) of Flupenthixol and immediately I felt sedated, so they lowered the dose to 25mg weekly, which seemed to suit me. But I still felt sedated and sleepy all the time.

Before I was put on a depot, my life was very hectic. I would be 'high' for a while, then would fall into a deep depression with suicidal tendencies. This was a pattern I followed for many years.

'I had given up smoking and was on track with my diet then
I eat four magnums one after the other. The diet

goes out the window in one foul swoop. Back to feeling shit
– yes it has reached my feet!! I turn into Hyde again.
All mixed up and angry. I turn into this monster wanting
To lash out at everything and destroy myself. I have to
Endure it till it goes on its own. And it does. It's just
Not very nice while I'm in it.'

Normality didn't come very often. I was either 'high' or 'low' with not much room in between. If I had a stable period, I would start a course or some other venture and get out and about. My 'high' allowed me to continue doing anything J planned to do because I never went 'over the top' by dancing over tables etc! My 'highs', were contained. I'd just get very excitable, talk a lot and spend money!! A pussy cat really.

I'm still feeling flat, trying to eat sensibly to shift the three
Pounds I put on. I did my shopping in a blur, just getting
Essentials for my diet. I feel like I'm walking with a lead
Weight on my head, crushing me and feeling dead inside.
I slept for four hours when I got in and at the moment, I'm
Listening to music which usually helps. My bed remains
Unmade and my curtains still drawn. I just threw on some
Clothes this morning to go out. Going about the motions
But feeling dead inside. My cats are miaowing around me.
It's like they sense I'm not right and just want reassurance.
They always get fed however I'm feeling, even if I don't
Feed myself.

I would go for my depot and watch the people coming in for theirs. They all looked like zombies, moving slowly, not speaking or engaging in conversation. I never wanted to be one of them, although I had no choice with the depot really. It was either that or a chaotic life and the main reason I wanted to try it was because of the overdoses. Having less pills indoors did help a bit.

Life on Flupenthixol was dull. My mood was like a mill pond. No variation in mood and I felt constantly flat, I told the staff time and time again that I didn't like the way it made me feel, but they never really listened to me, so I kept on it to keep the peace. I lost interest in most things I usually did before the depot and kept thinking of how busy I used to be. Now all I did when I was indoors was lay down because it made me sleepy all the time. I never felt like getting up in the mornings and remained subdued for the whole time I was on it.

I had a say on how much I had every week. The consultant wanted me on 75mg each week but that was too much for me, so it was lowered to 25mg, but I was never really happy with that. Because I never got angry, I didn't have the safety valve and the staff didn't realise I was getting depressed. They blamed it on losing my mum and said I was grieving but it was more than that.

My times at the local café got fewer and fewer and I had no conversation with anyone. I was missing the happy psychosis and 'highs' desperately but I didn't miss the bad psychosis which always followed. This was when I was out of touch with reality and began to be scared of everything, people mostly. I would avoid crowded places and avoided travelling on a bus during those times.

INSPIRATIONAL SONG

Mylie Cyrus – Nothing Breaks like a Heart.

Chapter Two
The Way it Is

My illness is very unpredictable. I never know from one day to the next how I'm going to be. It can be hard sometimes making plans for the future, as often I have to put things on hold.

Over the years, I have learnt to deal with most aspects of my Schitzo-affective Disorder. I said the other day that I wanted to work on the very low periods in my life, as I want to be able to manage that as well. It was pointed out to me that I have 'insight' for the majority of the time and can rationalise everything, but when I hit rock bottom all rationality and 'insight' gets swept away and I am at the mercy of the psychiatric services. As long as I continue to tell them what I plan on doing during those black times, the police will always find me and keep me safe.

It is those people who don't reach out during black phases that usually end up taking their own life. I have been in that situation many times, but one thing I am able to do is communicate my intentions and therefore keeping myself safe from serious harm and death.

This has been an exceptional stable period for me now, almost two months of stable mood and because of that I've been in the position to start making plans for my future. I know there will be further black periods when life feels intolerable, but I will face it when it happens, which it will at any time. As I've said, my illness is unpredictable but I face the rough with the smooth. I know the psychiatric services are there for me when I need them, and they can give me extra support as and when I need them. I feel reassured about this and safe in the knowledge that they will catch me when I fall. I don't have normality very often in my life and lately I've been a bit on the 'high' side but managing well.

After Christmas, everything fell a bit flat – there were no Christmas songs on the radio, and it seemed like things were slipping downwards. But I survived and as my support worker said, "It's natural to feel flat after the holidays." I bounced back now. I'm still getting my pills weekly and this seems to suit me fine.

My moods usually swing from 'high' to 'low' all the time, but I had an increase in my depot two months ago and I think this is why I'm more or less stable at the moment. I'm having weekly support with the psychiatric services but by the time I see someone ten days will have gone by, so I'm doing ok. Sometimes if I'm a bit 'high', I've taken extra medication at night, so that I can get a good night's sleep.

'Today I received a card. It had Aunty Stephanie
On the envelope. Thinking it was from my nephews,
I opened it but it was a letter from my sister. Decided
Not to read it. It would only have brought me down'.

I'm not a bad person, but they make me feel bad about myself and it's easy just accept it rather than fight it. But I'm a survivor. I've survived many low times in my life. I have to protect number one because no one else is going to do it for me! I've survived criticism and prejudice. I've survived suicide attempts. Sometimes it feels like I'm taking on the world but every time I come out of it fighting. I've been fighting all my life. Now it's time for some harmony and enjoyment. Vernon makes me happy. We spend time together. I tell him I'm going to marry him one day, even if it takes five years! He said on my birthday that he loved me a bit. I replied by saying, "I love you a bit too and you've just made my birthday and Christmas all in one."

If Vernon and I were to get married, we'd need a big house with plenty of room so that he could have his own space and I could have mine. Both our flats are too small to survive in. Vernon says, "If we have a big house, it would have to have a secret compartment." I don't know where he thinks we're going to live – in a castle?! Anyway, we can dream at least. We could decide not to get married but just live together. It's taken three years for us to get slightly closer to each other (that being a kiss or a hug or holding hands) that it will probably take another three years to have a serious relationship with each other. He's very secretive about his flat and doesn't like many visitors, so will just have to be patient. He's had a few serious relationships in the past and so have I, but we've both been badly hurt, so it's going to take some time.

Chapter Three
A Little Further Along

'It's been a week since the depression took a hold
On me again, but I seem to be coming out of the
Blackness now. The light is beginning to shine again
And I can see a way forward. I just pick up from where
I left off and carry on. That's what I always do. Time
And time again. Things seem alien – my flat, the cats,
Where I live, the shops that I frequent. It's like I've
Been away but not in a nice place. It's been very dark
And there seemed to be no escape.

When the sun shines again, it's like I have to celebrate life all over again and being alive. It's like life stops during those times, I can't think straight and am dependent on the mental health services. Sometimes they help. Sometimes I'm better on my own because only I know how it feels.

During the time I was on Flupenthixol, I saw this fella from time to time. I've known him for about twenty years, but he always had a drink problem when we occasionally met up for a coffee. He'd seen me when I'd been depressed and 'high' and always said, "You are still you however you are." He offered me comfort sometimes but because of his drinking, I never got close to him. Then I lost contact with him for quite a while and found out much later that he had been in a secure unit for alcohol poisoning and that he nearly died. Then one day I saw him, and he told me he was now free from drink.

We started meeting up on a Saturday at the local market café and to be honest, he was a joy to be around. One year led to two and I bought him a congratulations card each year he was dry. He told me no one else had done that for him and was very grateful that I was acknowledging his achievements. It is now three years since he stopped drinking and I bought him another card.

Since he stopped drinking, we have got closer and I am very fond of him. He makes me laugh and I feel comfortable in his company. We've been out for the odd meal together and just recently went to the pictures. Sometimes if I am depressed, I wouldn't meet him, but ring him when I felt all right again.

INSPIRATIONAL SONGS

Shirley Bassey – Something
Cilla Black – Anyone had a Heart
Carpenters – I know I Need to be in Love

'I've decided the time is right to go back to
Bereavement counselling. I have deep seated
Loss for my friend more so than for my mum for
Whom I loved dearly, but she never really understood
Me, even though I think at times she tried. My friend
Understood me and time after time she would forgive
Me for getting angry with her during my depressions.'

We would fall out briefly. This happened often and at the time of her untimely death, we had been apart for a couple of months. Had we been seeing each other, I wonder sometimes if she would still be with us.

'It's no use thinking 'what ifs', she's dead and no amount of
reassurance will bring her back to life again. It just
Makes me think how precious life is.'

I think the last time I was depressed, it didn't last as long
as usual. The realisation that I will come out of it is beginning
to sink in at long last.

'It's the pits when I'm depressed and I want 'out', usually
Getting angry with myself and wanting to self-destruct.'

The anger and destruction are only there because there
seems no better place to be and it's better to be angry than
accept a depression that hits rock bottom for no apparent
reason.

'Why should I be depressed when I have
Everything going for me. Surely looking forward
To voluntary work should be enough to stop it
In its tracks.'

But once it gets a hold on me, I just have to wait for it to
disperse and disappear, which is usually does.

Just recently, I became very unwell, psychotic and
depressed. I was in crisis and eventually seen by the
Psychiatrist. I told him I was unhappy on the Flupenthixol and
could he put me on something less sedating. He agreed and
started me on Aripiprazole tablets, 10 mg daily. I was on that
for two weeks and then he put the dose up to 15mg. At the end
of the two weeks, I was started on a new depot of Aripiprazole

300mg. I still complained of feeling sedated, but he assured me it was less sedating. I couldn't quite believe him at the time. He then stopped the tablets and I waited for the depot to take effect.

The depot from hell
Flupenthixol
Dulling everything around me
Leaving me dead inside
Time for change
The depot of choice
Aripiprazole
A new beginning
A new start
A life

While my mother was dying, I chose to stay away. I couldn't deal with the fact that she had lost the power of speech following a stroke and was unable to communicate with anyone.

This must have been very frustrating for her and I couldn't bear to see her like that. I was unpopular with some of my siblings but had to protect myself. I thought about her often during those weeks but didn't see her until after she had passed away, the morning of her funeral. Although she had died, I felt her spirit with me in the room as I said my goodbyes. I have felt it since then and hardly a day goes by without a thought of her.

Following my first depot, a strange thing happened. I went 'high' for the first time in eighteen months and suddenly I had loads of energy and didn't feel like sleeping all the time. I didn't feel tired for sleep or hungry for food, but I forced myself to bed each night and to eat regularly.

Rainbows of colour
Strips of light
Across the sky
A wonderful sight
Full of delight

High like a bird
Flying in the sky
Wings outstretched
Drifting along
Without a care in the world

Following from the 'high' I became psychotic and was frightened of everything, especially people and situations. I was 'high' one minute then 'low' then scared. This went on all weekend and I lost count of how many times I rang the crisis line.

'Once again, I've surfaced from a depressive phase which
Lasted a couple of weeks. It's funny how I feel
The strength come from my toes to my head and
I'm able to function.'

I then arrange to meet my fella who I probably haven't seen for a while. I don't like him seeing me when I'm down – it's no fun for him and I wouldn't want to burden him.

'Hey what – back I've gone into another spiralling
Downward trend. For no apparent reason. It just
Keeps happening. I'm either 'high' or I'm 'low'
With nothing in between.'

While I'm down, I just want 'out' but I hang on to the
thought that I'll come out of it again.

I saw my Care co-ordinator and she saw the other side of
me being 'flat'.

'I've put my meds outside again to keep
Them out of reach while I'm down.'

INSPIRATIONAL SONG

Elton John – I'm still Standing

A sudden sound
A rush to the light
A moment of panic
A moment of peace
Peace perfect peace

Within two doses of a second anti-psychotic, I didn't feel
scared anymore. The consultant said he would keep me on the
tablets as well as the depot from now on.

'I've crashed again. Have cancelled the rest of my
Course and deferred the Health and Social care
One for another time. Yesterday was dreadful.
I was thinking how to snuff it but today I've turned
A corner yet again.'

In tough times
I seek refuge
From the outside world
Hidden from view
In the comfort of solitude
Until the light appears again
And it always does

'Three weeks have gone by and I feel so much
better if not a little 'high' at times. My
Interests have all come back and I feel like
Myself again, bubbly and chatty, engaging
With people and doing some water colour
Paintings. I feel alive. My head is clear and
Not cluttered anymore.'

Chapter Four
A New Day – A New Challenge

When I think back to the previous eighteen months that I've had, I realise that I was like dead inside with no feelings or emotions. The Flupenthixol took that all away. If I could get everyone off that drug, I would. It is soul destroying and shouldn't be licenced.

My life has turned a corner and only because I was persistent in my quest for a change. It took a while but finally I was listened to and the rest is history. I'm happy (if not a little 'high' at times) but I've got feelings back and also my drive to succeed. All my hobbies have come back to me and I'm actually enjoying life and feel at peace.

'I'm actually looking forward to my first book
Getting on the shelves in shops. It took ten
Years to come to fruition but it was worth all
The hard work. I feel proud of what I've
Achieved even if I say so myself!'

My new Care co-ordinator is lovely. She is down to earth and on my first appointment she told me she was firm but wouldn't tell me what to do. (I hate being told what to do – I'd rather do something and make my own mistakes and learn from it).

'I think we're going to have a good
Working relationship.'

Because of the Schitzo-affective Disorder, I will always be on the books and won't be discharged to the care of my GP like many others I know. I've been under the mental health services for forty years and I've come a long way since those early years. I'm looking forward to a brighter future.

I'm going to be working as a peer support worker for MIND (a mental health charity) shortly and I can't wait to get started. I think with all my experience I'll have lots to offer others in a similar position. I would like to help others get to a place they feel comfortable in their own skin – make them shine.

Chapter Five
My 'Highs'

When I am 'high', I can achieve anything and my optimism grows. I have loads of energy, am very chatty and bubbly and enjoy painting in water colour and socialising. I fill up my days (if I didn't have a diary, I wouldn't be able to remember everything I pack into my days and week).

I usually apply to do various courses and am tempted to try paid employment, but I am very wary of doing this because I know how horribly wrong it can turn out, so I stay on benefits and stay safe. My excitement levels are raised and simple pleasures feel like I'm on cloud nine! I talk fast, changing from one subject to another rapidly. I can get agitated if things don't go my way.

I only socialise with energetic people. I have no time for moaners and people complaining about the price of a loaf of bread! I keep my diary full. I can over do things and have to be reminded to rest occasionally to stop burning out. I do this reluctantly but it's a good tool to have. I am very optimistic about my future and start planning ahead. I write loads of things to read out at my sessions with the psychiatric services, but during these times I have little contact with them. I don't need them – I'm fine and well!

This good phase can last anything from a few days to several weeks. Friends and acquaintances remark on how well I am. My face is radiant with a constant smile. I wear makeup every day and usually wear dresses or skirts as opposed to jeans and jumpers.

I can get psychosis during this time but it's a happy psychosis where I dream up all sorts of scenarios. Once, I fell in love with my consultant and started bombarding him with love letters. I was getting messages off of the radio telling me he loved me, but in reality it was all in my head – a figment of my imagination.

I can survive on very little sleep. I usually have to take extra medication during these times to get enough sleep. I'd stay up all night if I could, but I know this will just push my mood up even higher! I feel my mood elevating inside. It goes from my waist to the tip of my head.

Usually when I'm like this, I have another go at giving up smoking. I find it much easier to quit when everything in my life is so great and exciting. I'm usually very successful too.

'It's day two of quit smoking and
Doing well.'

INSPIRATIONAL SONGS

Mylie Cyrus – The Climb
Carpenters – Top of the world

Chapter Six
Trying to Move Forward

'Home life has much improved. I actually
Enjoy being indoors and not too concerned
About visiting my neighbour like I was.'

There was a time when I hated my own company and my flat got very messy and uncared for. I didn't hoover for weeks and bearing in mind I have two cats – the cat hair was everywhere, my bed remained unchanged and washing up was piling up. Now everything is ship shape, the hoovering gets done twice a week and I'm taking a pride in my surroundings.

'I've been wearing make-up every day for
Three weeks which is good – just a little bit of
Eye shadow, mascara, a sweep of blusher on
My cheeks and lipstick.'

I take my last pill at eight o clock so am usually ready for bed by nine. This means I get up really early – about three-thirty, but I've had seven hours sleep by then, so I'm ready to get up.

'I actually feel like getting up now and
Look forward to each new day. My diary
Is full and I'm kept really busy which is good.'

I enjoy visiting my favourite café and sitting outside to watch the world go by. I enjoy chatting to people as they pass by and smile readily at people.

'I love life now and am looking forward
To my week away to Cornwall.'

It's a caravan holiday and I'm going back to the same site I have been to many times. The small town is lovely with quaint little shops to get gifts in. There are plenty of places to eat and drink and I enjoy nothing more than sitting outside and watch the world go by. I always go on my own – that way I can please myself where I go with no one to answer to. There are always people to chat to both on and off site and I usually have a good time.

'I have some lovely plants on my
Balcony which I'm caring for, geraniums
And a small hydrangea. They get
Watered every day. I did grow some seeds
But they all died. What a waste of money!'

Chapter Seven
My 'Lows'

I feel my mood drop from the tip of my head. Generally, when this feeling reaches my shoulders, I start making noises to the psychiatric services, saying that my mood is slipping and basically 'HELP ME'. Sometimes this feeling rests on my shoulders and doesn't go any further. This is manageable. My 'insight' is still intact and I can continue functioning. If it reaches my waist, I'm in trouble because it's only a matter of time before it reaches my feet – then I'm in turmoil. I lose all 'insight' and rationality. Once it gathers momentum, there's no turning back and no matter what I'm doing or what's happening in my life (especially good things) my mood just plummets.

As it reaches my feet, I'm in a black hole with no light to be seen. I want to self-destruct and voice things like, 'I'm going to the beach and I'm going to just head for the water – the water will swallow me up and I'll be finished – out of my torment, out of my pain and misery.'

Luckily, I always voice these intentions and many times when I've felt that 'low' and intent on killing myself, I get found by the police and they take me to a place of safety. I see only black, wear no make-up, stop going out, stop bathing and cleaning my teeth. Life just stops.

I can't think straight – in fact my only thought is how am I going to do it!

My consultant is wise to my suicide attempts with my medication and now instructs the pharmacy to issue seven tablets at a time, one for each night. This has been the case for several months now and I know that if I took seven tablets all at once, it wouldn't kill me – well maybe not!

All my plans have to take a back burner until I come out of it – which I always do. When I'm 'low' and have given up smoking, I usually gravitate back to tobacco again. I find it a crutch on which to lean on.

During my 'low' moods, I avoid eye contact and look at the ground. In my mind, it makes me invisible, and I feel no one can see me. I hate these times. I hate the way it makes me feel and all life stops for a while.

I still frequent cafés when 'low' but don't communicate with anyone. As I said, I look at the floor. My theory is 'if I can't see them, they can't see me.' My face gives the game away – my whole face drops to a grimace. I look deep in thought but in reality, I'm not feeling anything except empty and desperate. I get comfort listening to all the chit chat going on even though I'm not engaging.

I can be like this for weeks at a time. People who know me well know I can't help how I feel and they just leave me alone. While I am in this desperate state, I have more contact with the mental health services, Safe Haven and Crisis team. They know me very well and know that when I ring them it is urgent. Sometimes I just break down and cry without saying anything, but just knowing someone is on the other end of the phone is a huge comfort.

Chapter Eight
Going Forward

There had been some changes within the mental health services and because I was with a particular surgery, faced a move to a different area. This would mean a change of Care coordinator and a new consultant. I don't always fair well with change, but I was optimistic when I met my new Care co-ordinator. She was very nice, and I seemed to gel well with her. But I took a turn for the worst, and this was when my trouble started.

'I feel 'low', I think I'll ring someone.'

When I rang the new team, I told them I was in crisis and was in need of support. Because I was new to them, they were slow to react and after ringing four times gave up and took matters into my own hands.

'Why haven't they rung me? Oh, sod it.
I can't handle this anymore!'

I promptly took an overdose of my prescription drugs and intended just going to bed, but after a while I started to feel unwell and staggered up the road to the Safe Haven. They didn't open till six pm and although I told them I'd taken an overdose, said they couldn't let me in because it was too early.

I took this as a sign that they didn't want to help me, so staggered to a local taxi firm and got in a taxi to the local A&E Department. On the way there, I could feel my heart racing and was beginning to think it would be too late for help. The taxi driver helped me into the department. It was heaving with people. I then had to wait four hours to be assessed. There were staff around so felt sure that if I collapsed, they would deal with me. I was in their hands really.

'I've done it again! Why do I put myself
Through this time and time again! I never Learn!!'

Eventually, I was seen and after an ECG and blood tests, was moved to an assessment ward.

Even though I was in a fragile state, I wanted to leave but was told that I had to see the doctor and be seen by the mental health team. They kept me waiting and I tried again to leave but this time they said, "If you leave, we'll involve the police and they will find you and bring you back." This stopped me in my tracks, so patiently waited to be seen. When I was seen, they asked me if I intended to kill myself.

I replied, "No." I was just trying to get some help for myself, but my plea was ignored. After about twenty hours I was deemed fit to leave so I got another taxi home supplied with a week's supply of medication, as I had taken all that I had.

When I got home, I decided as a precaution, to lock all my meds in my outside cupboard for safe keeping, just taking out what I needed for the night.

The next day, my new team sprang into action and promptly saw me and put me on 'shared Care' for the interim period. I still wasn't happy as this all could have been avoided. If it had been my old team, they would have known straight away that I needed help as they knew me very well and could recognise the signs in me and act accordingly.

A few days later, I decided to find out which surgeries were under my old team. This I did and found another surgery, registered and three days later was back under my old team. I was to carry on seeing the same Care co-ordinator until a replacement could be found, so was happy with that. We had recently completed another crisis plan in which I choose how I wish to be treated when in crisis – the main thing is they just support me and don't take over my life.

'My mood has been level for a week now.
I seem to be picking up again. Could be
Heading for a 'high' now but it hasn't happened.'

My mood has been steady for a while now and I've continued to have support by my Care co-ordinator. She was sorry that things hadn't worked out well for me but felt I had the right to change if that was what I wanted.

'I thought I was heading for a 'low',
But I'm OK.'

INSPIRATIONAL SONGS

Shirley Bassey – Send in the Clowns
Abba – I have a Dream

Chapter Nine
Another Day

'I'm still waiting to hear about voluntary
Work with MIND. The advert has got to go in
First, then I'll be sent an application form. I'm
Getting fed up with waiting! But that's me all
Over – if someone says they're going to do
Something, I expect them to do it. I'll just have
To be patient! Patience isn't my strong point!'

When I saw my Care co-ordinator, I told her I was stable, but since then I'd noticed I'd gone off watching all my DVD's and my choice of music had changed. I was listening to melancholy music instead of up lifting music. This was usually an indicator that my mood was dropping. Also, I was going back to bed instead of staying up.

'Will keep a close eye on things.'
The following morning, I got up and
Stayed up, so I'm doing OK'

I'd planned to do some decorating in my living room. I was going from green to pink, so promptly got the paint and started clearing the room. My flat looked like a junk heap as I moved everything out and putting it all in a different room. It had been a while since I'd done any decorating but was confident I could do a good job and save myself some money!

It took me three days to complete but I was pleased with the end result. The walls needed three coats of paint to cover the green. I was soon putting everything back and admired my handy work. The cats were a bit bemused by all the activity but were fine and didn't end up with wet paint on themselves!

'My holiday is getting closer and I'm actually
Looking forward to it, knowing that my health has
Improved. My depot is due just before I go.'

It'll take about six hours to get to Cornwall by train, but I actually enjoy the journey through a lot of countryside. People say to me, "How could you go away on your own?" But I always have. I suppose there's never been anyone I'd like to spend a week with. I gave my fella the offer to come with me but he declined saying he'd worry about his flat while he was away. I know Pickles and Asher will be fine with my neighbour. He enjoys spending time with them, plus I've got more channels on the TV than he has, so he spends a lot of time in mine. I don't mind though. I usually leave him money in case of emergencies and give him some for his time.

INSPIRATIONAL SONG

Carpenters – Make believe it's your first time

Chapter Ten
A New Challenge – Again!

I've been looking forward to seeing my cousin again. She's been away on holiday with friends and I've really missed her. I expect she's got lots of photos to show me and I'm looking forward to hearing all about her time away. I didn't get a postcard though!

Apart from my cousin and a couple of aunties, there's not anyone else I'm close to except my fella. I get on really well with him, but we haven't got to the stage of having relations with each other. It's never really come to that – we're just good friends. I know a lot of people around the area where I live and I'm on speaking terms with all of them, but I don't live in any of their pockets!

'My balcony is looking very pretty with plenty
Of flowers and it's a pleasure to sit out there
And admire all my hard work. It's good for the
Soul to have something pretty to look at.'

I decided to go along to the Bench Theatre (an amateur dramatics group). I was a member several years ago but I think my health wasn't very good, so I left. Now I've decided to re-join to do 'behind the scenes' and I'm paid up till next year. Everyone was so pleased to see me and it was a jolly evening. They don't meet up again till later in the year, so will go along when they return.

> 'I've been a bit 'high' for a few days but
> It's no problem. I've just got loads of
> Energy to do things. I've enjoyed being
> In today, listening to my music as usual.
> The cats are asleep after their food.'

I had a lovely relaxing time on holiday in Cornwall. My caravan was well equipped with everything I needed. I spent my time reading (finished three books and had to buy another!) I treated myself to two pictures of Looe which I have put in my living room. I went into Looe every day and did the same thing each time – sitting outside a café drinking tea, having a meander in all the little shops, then finishing off with either chips or an ice cream by the sea front.

I had been feeling a bit down when I went but that improved as the days went by, so by the time I got home I felt fine. My cats and my neighbour were glad to see me home safe and sound.

I'm now looking forward to going to Jersey next month. It's an organised coach holiday. I've never been to Jersey, so am looking forward to it.

Chapter Eleven
Sunshine and Rainbows

I am about to start voluntary work for the Safe Haven. It is Peer support work, offering guidance and support to people coming to the centre. My role will involve listening to clients concerns and if they wish, share my own experiences of how I have learnt to cope with different aspects of my mental health.

My boss will be monitoring me and I will have the chance to 'off load' to her if anything triggering happens, during the course of my shift. Together, we have put a 'wellbeing package' in place for me, so that if I'm going through a rough patch and unable to work, I can still access the Safe Haven, when the clients have left. I told her I've got things indoors to 'self sooth', that being cross stitch, reading or listening to music.

I am looking forward to starting as soon as possible, but at the moment I'm waiting for my DBS check to come back, because I will be working with vulnerable adults. Also, I have approached the Recovery College, with a view to joining them in the near future. They put on courses to do with managing your mental health and have been a regular student over the years, doing courses in Self Esteem, Managing Crisis and many more. They do courses locally and I'm sure they will be interested in having me on board.

After I have been doing the Peer Support work for a while,

I asked about the possibility of increasing my hours and eventually, I would like to do a shift doing face to face work with clients in crisis. I have a mountain of experience with my own mental health and have learnt to cope with changes in my mood, sometimes on a daily basis. At this point of writing, my health is very good, and I am optimistic about the future.

I am about to do two book sales of my first book, 'And I'm Still Waiting', for charity. Also, I am doing a sale of some of my paintings for charity. I have accumulated quite a few over the years and would just like a good home for them all.

Sometimes when I am well, I think about paid work, but I know that always goes badly wrong so probably won't. Sometimes having a fulfilling life can be enough to satisfy me, but I'm always envious of those people who can hold down a job without even thinking about it.

Do you remember me talking about going to Jersey? Well, I went and although I was 'high' all week, had a lovely time. The hotel was very nice. It was three star but more like a five star hotel. Everyone was so friendly. I met this chap who was also on his own, so I invited him to join me on my table, rather than us both sitting on our own. He was very much like me – liked his own space and doing his own thing, but we got on very well. We exchanged addresses and phone numbers, but since being back we have only had contact once. I plan to go back to Jersey in 2024.

In May 2023, I go to Spain for 10 days. I've had to take out extra insurance because of my mental health and have covered al eventualities, so if I am ill I can get back quickly. It's an organised coach holiday and we'll be moving around Spain, staying in three hotels and finishing off in Paris for the last night. I am looking forward to going so hope I stay well.

Usually, I dread Christmas as I'm normally on my own, but this year I invited some friends round on Christmas Eve. It went really well, and we all had a lovely time. Christmas day I was on my own, but the radio played lots of Christmas songs and I got through it. It was very uplifting listening to all the old favourites that pop up year after year. My neighbour and I exchanged presents on Christmas morning. I'd bought a large stocking for him, filled to the brim with lots of goodies. He bought me some lovely gifts too, so all in all a lovely day. I think having my friends around on Christmas eve was a brilliant idea and one I shall think of again next year without fail.

Chapter Twelve
And to Finish

'I've finally surfaced again. I'm getting
Back to my old self. I think my holiday
Had a lot to do with it. I really chilled
Out and did nothing but read, eat cream
Teas and listening to music. A perfect Combination!'

I'm truly grateful to my consultant and his team for listening to me two months ago.

Although I am still going 'high' and 'low', I genuinely feel much happier since I've been on the Aripiprazole. Now all I have to cope with is the ups and downs but without the sedating feeling of the Flupenthixol. I enjoy being busy and having things to look forward to.

I did wonder if an increase in the depot would stop me going so 'high' and therefore not falling quite so much afterwards. I have mentioned this to my consultant and am waiting to hear from her.

I have just heard that my new Care co-ordinator is someone I have seen before, so I'm delighted about that. She is lovely and we got on really well before so that can only continue again.

I think myself lucky that my physical health is good even though my mental health is a challenge sometimes. The majority of the time I am busy doing various things but sometimes I have to cancel what I'm doing until a better time.

Life continues to be a battle of wits with the 'highs' and 'lows', but it doesn't stop me from making the best of a life!

<u>Methods I use for self soothing</u>

I enjoy going to a café and watching the world go by, staying in the here and now. It's a great way to unwind and you can generally see all sorts of people going about their everyday business. I often wonder what they're thinking about as they go about their day.

Other practices I have include listening to the radio or putting a record or CD on. I have a wide range of music to suit every mood. When I am angry, I like to play Bohemium Rhapsody at full blast. I pity my neighbours, but in all the years I have lived here they haven't once complained about the loud music. Anyway, after half an hour, I've got it out of my system and turned it down!

My water colour paints come out from time to time. It's very relaxing just watching the brush strokes on the canvas and seeing what I can create.

I keep a journal and diary and write in it every day. It's useful to notice if my mood has dipped and by writing it down, I can keep tabs on it. It's very therapeutic to write, I feel. I write all my thoughts down and sometimes just writing it all down helps to unravel the chaos in my head.

I also enjoy a bit of gardening and usually have some pretty flowers on my balcony to look at. At the moment, the daffodils are beginning to come up and they are so joyful when they open up and lovely in colour.

I'm an avid reader. I like autobiographies and have read many, including Dame Judy Dench, Julie Walters, Elton John and many more. It's nice to know how the other half lives and it's just interesting reading. Recently I read 'Eat, Pray, Love' by Elizabeth Gilbert. It's about a woman going through a divorce and other failed relationships. She visits an Ashram in India and through meditation finds herself again. It made me think I'd like to try meditation as a way of coping, so will go to the library and get a book about it. There's no harm in trying!

GENERAL RIGHTS

I have the right to express myself provided I do not set out to hurt or put others down in the process

So does everyone else.

I have the right to be treated with respect as an intelligent, capable and equal human being

So does everyone else.

I have the right to state my own needs and priorities as a person whatever people expect of me because of my roles in life

So does everyone else.

I have the right to deal with people without having to make them like or approve of me

So does everyone else.

I have the right to ask for what I want

So does everyone else.

I have the right to say 'yes' or 'no' for myself

So does everyone else.

I have the right to change my mind

So does everyone else.

I have the right to say 'I don't understand'

So does everyone else.

I AM ME
My Declaration of Self Esteem

In all the world, there is no one else exactly like me. Everything that comes out of me is authentically mine because I alone chose it. I own everything about me, my body, my feelings, my mouth, my voice, all my actions, whether they be to others or to myself. I own my fantasies, my dreams, my hopes, my fears. I own all my triumphs and successes, all my failures and mistakes. Because I own all of me, I can become intimately acquainted with me. By so doing, I can love me and be friendly with me in all my parts. I know there are aspects about myself that puzzle me, and other aspects that I do not know. But as long as I am friendly and loving to myself, I can courageously and hopefully look for solutions to the puzzles and for ways to find out more about me. However I look, and sound, whatever I say and do, and whatever I think and feel at a given moment in time is authentically me. If later some parts of how I looked, sounded, thought and felt turn out to be unfitting, I can discard that which is unfitting, keep the rest and invent something new for that which I discarded. I can see, hear, feel, think, say and do. I have the tools to survive, to be close to others, to be productive, and to make sense and order out of the world, of people and things outside of me. I own me, and therefore I can engineer me. I am me and I AM OKAY....

What is Schizoaffective Disorder

Schizoaffective Disorder is a mental illness that can affect your thoughts, mood and behaviour. You may have symptoms of bipolar and schizophrenia. These symptoms may be mania (high mood), depression (low mood) and psychosis (losing touch with reality. About 1 in 200 people develop schizoaffective disorder at some time during their life. It tends to develop during early adulthood and is more common in women than men.

Schizoaffective Disorder has symptoms of schizophrenia and bipolar. You can experience psychosis with mania and depression. No one knows what causes Schizoaffective Disorder. Research shows that genetic and environmental factors can increase your risk of getting this Illness.

Diagnosis and Symptoms

A psychiatrist will diagnose Schizoaffective Disorder after a mental health assessment. It might take more than one assessment for the psychiatrist to reach a diagnosis. You may get a diagnosis of Schizoaffective Disorder if you have depressive or mania symptoms with symptoms of schizophrenia. To get a diagnosis of Schizoaffective Disorder, you should have had a combination of symptoms of both psychosis and bipolar disorder. Your symptoms should be clearly there for at least two weeks.

Symptoms of Schizophrenia

Schizophrenia is a mental illness which affects the way you think. Symptoms can affect how you cope with day to day life. Symptoms include:-

Hallucinations – you may hear, see or feel things that aren't there.

Delusions – you may believe things that aren't true

Disorganised speech – you may begin to talk quickly or slowly an things you say may not make sense to other people. You may switch topics with no obvious link.

Disorganised Behaviour – you might struggle to organise your life or stick to appointments etc.

Catatonic Behaviour – you may feel unable to move or appear to be in a daze.

Negative symptoms – these are symptoms that involve loss of ability and enjoyment in life

They can include the following things:-

Lack of motivation

Change in sleep patterns

Poor grooming or hygiene

Difficulty in planning and setting goals

Not saying much

Change in body language

Lack of eye contact

Reduced range of emotions

Less interest in socialising or hobbies and activities

Low sex drive

What are the symptoms of Mania

You may experience the following if you have mania:-

Feeling overly active or energetic or restless

Feeling more irritable than usual

Feeling overly confident

Talking very quickly, jumping from one idea to another or having racing thoughts

Feeling elated, even if things are not going well for you

Being easily distracted and struggling to focus on one topic

Not needing much sleep

Thinking you can do more than you can, which could lead to risky situations and behaviour

Doing things you wouldn't normally which can cause problems, such as spending lots of money, having casual sex with different partners, using drugs or alcohol, gambling or making unwise business decisions

Being much more social than usual

Being argumentative, pushy or aggressive

Mania is associated with Bipolar Disorder.

What are the symptoms of Depression

You may experience the following:-

Low mood

Less energy, tired or 'slowed down'

Hopeless or negative

Guilty, worthless or helpless

Less interested in things you normally like to do

Difficulty concentrating, remembering or making decisions

Restless or irritable

Sleep too much, not being able to sleep or have disturbed sleep

More of less hungry than usual or have a weight change

Thoughts of death or suicide or attempted suicide

Types and Causes

There are three different types of Schizoaffective Disorder.

What is the manic type?

This means you have symptoms of schizophrenia and mania at the same time through a period of illness.

What is the depressive type?

This means you have symptoms of schizophrenia and depression at the same time through a period of illness.

What is mixed type?

This means you have symptoms of schizophrenia, depression and mania at the same time through a period of illness.

What causes Schizoaffective Disorder?

Psychiatrists don't know precisely what causes Schizoaffective Disorder, but we do know that you will have a chemical imbalance in your brain if you have the condition.

Research shows that genetic and environmental factors can increase your risk of developing the illness.

Genetic Factors

Schizoaffective Disorder is slightly more common if other

members of your family have Schizophrenia, Schizoaffective Disorder of Bipolar Disorder.

Environmental Factors

These are your personal experiences. It is thought that stress can contribute towards a schizoaffective episode. Stress can be caused by many things such as bereavement, debt or employment problems. Childhood trauma can also be a factor in the condition developing in later life. Research suggests that bad treatment in your childhood can make psychosis more likely.

Who will manage my treatment

Different mental health teams can support and treat you.

Referrals

A doctor can refer you to a mental health professional if deemed necessary or you can refer yourself.

What is an NHS Community Mental Health Team (CMHT)?

This is a team of professionals who support you to recover from mental health issues. They can give short or long-term care in the community.

What is an NHS Crisis Team?

They can support you if you are having a crisis in the community. They can offer short-term support to help prevent hospital admissions. They can arrange for you to go to hospital if you are very unwell.

You can get crisis support by:-

Calling your NHS urgent mental health helpline

Calling NHS 111 or

Talking to your GP

Further reading

Wellness Recovery Action Plan (WRAP) plus

This is a self-designed wellness process. You can use a WRAP to get well, stay well and make your life your own. It was developed in 1997 by a group of people who were searching for ways of coping with their own lives and fulfilling dreams and ambitions.

USEFUL CONTACTS

The hearing voices network

Support and understanding for those who hear voices or experience other types of hallucination.

Address:- 86-90 Paul Street, London, EC2A 4NE

Email:- info@hearing-voices.org

Website:- www.hearing-voices.org

Risks that Schizoaffective Disorder can cause

Suicide risk is higher for the few years after symptoms start. You can seek treatment early and make a crisis plan. The right treatment can help control your symptoms and help lower the risk of suicide.

You can make a crisis plan yourself or ask someone to help you. This will help to deal with suicidal thoughts. Usually a plan includes people, services and activities that can help you.

CARERS

If you are a carer, you can get support if you care for someone with schizoaffective disorder.

Here are some options:-

Family intervention through NHS

Join a carers service

Ask your local authority for a carers assessment

Read about the condition

Apply for welfare benefits for carers

Rethink Mental Illness run carers support groups in some areas.

Also search for groups on the Carers Trust website.

Rethink Mental Illness www.rethink.org/about-us/our-support-groups

Carers Trust:- www.carers.0rg/search//netw0rk-partners